Are You a True Disciple?

Are You a True Disciple?

by
John MacArthur, Jr.

MOODY PRESS
CHICAGO

All Scripture quotations in chapters 1-3, unless noted otherwise, are from
the *New Scofield Reference Bible*, King James Version. All Scripture quotations in chapter 4, unless noted otherwise, are from the *New American Stan-
dard Bible*. Copyright © 1967 by Oxford University Press, Inc. Reprinted by
permission.

ISBN: 0-8024-5341-4

1 2 3 4 5 6 Printing/LC/Year 94 93 92 91 90

Printed in the United States of America

Contents

These Bible studies are taken from messages delivered by Pastor-Teacher John MacArthur, Jr., at Grace Community Church in Panorama City, California. The recorded messages themselves may be purchased as a series or individually. Please request the current price list by writing to:

"GRACE TO YOU"
P.O. Box 4000
Panorama City, CA 91412

Or call the following toll-free number:
1-800-55-GRACE

1
Divine Sorrow over Spiritual Defection

Outline

Introduction

Lesson
 I. Israel's Spiritual Defection
   A. As Seen in Exodus
   B. As Seen in the Psalms
   C. As Seen in Isaiah
   D. As Seen in Jeremiah
 II. God's Sorrow over Spiritual Defection
   A. Revealed Through Jeremiah
   B. Revealed Through Christ
     1. He wept over Jerusalem
     2. He was forsaken by His followers

Introduction

It grieves God's heart when people make a superficial commitment to Him and then bail out. Unfortunately, that kind of spiritual defection has been a common occurrence since the beginning of time and continues today. Defection is desertion from an allegiance or loyalty. We have all experienced it to one extent or another. People have dealt treacherously with us—perhaps even a close friend whom we had loved and poured our lives into. Nothing is more painful than that kind of betrayal, and no wound is as deep as when someone defects from an intimate relationship. And the more we have invested spiritually in that person, the greater the pain.

Heaven also feels pain regarding someone's spiritual defection. God's heart is broken by those who follow Him for a brief time with no more than superficial commitment, then forsake Him when they don't get what they expected.

Lesson

I. ISRAEL'S SPIRITUAL DEFECTION

During Old Testament times many people in the nation of Israel were not true worshipers of God. Outwardly, they were identified with God's people, but inwardly they had defected from Him.

A. As Seen in Exodus

Exodus 32 gives the tragic account of the golden calf. While Moses was on Mount Sinai receiving the law from God, his brother, Aaron, was leading the people in idolatrous worship. So the Lord said to Moses, "Go, get thee down; for thy people, whom thou broughtest out of the land of Egypt, have corrupted themselves. They have turned aside quickly out of the way which I commanded them: they have made a melted calf, and have worshiped it, and have sacrificed thereunto, and said, These are thy gods, O Israel, which have brought thee up out of the land of Egypt. And the Lord said unto Moses, I have seen this people, and, behold, it is a stiff-necked people. Now therefore let me alone, that my wrath may burn against them, and I may consume them: and I will make of thee a great nation" (vv. 7-10). God's reaction expressed the conflicting emotions of His wounded heart: He wanted to destroy His people for their disobedience, but He was still willing to fulfill His promise to make a great nation of Abraham's descendants through Moses (Gen. 12:2).

B. As Seen in the Psalms

In Psalm 18:21 David writes, "I have kept the ways of the Lord, and have not wickedly departed from my God." He was implying that many of his contemporaries had depart-

8

ed from God. Throughout the Old Testament the story of Israel is one of shallow commitment and spiritual defection. The people God loved caused Him tremendous sorrow, deserting Him again and again.

The Tears God Shed over a Pagan Nation

God's sorrow over spiritual defection is so great that He wept even for Moab, a pagan nation adjacent to Israel. While pronouncing judgment on the country for its evil, God said, "Therefore I will bewail. . . . I will water thee with my tears" (Isa. 16:9). He also said, "My heart shall sound like an harp for Moab" (Isaiah 16:11), meaning it would play a melancholy tune. Even though God didn't have a covenantal relationship with Moab, that nation deserted Him in the sense that all unregenerates do: they refused to acknowledge the God they knew they were accountable to (cf. Rom. 1:19-23). And since God is a person, He feels the pain of desertion.

C. As Seen in Isaiah

1. Isaiah 5:1-7—God says, "Now will I sing to my well-beloved a song." He then used the analogy of a vineyard that brought forth bad grapes to describe Israel's defection from Him. In verse 4 He says, "What could have been done more to my vineyard, that I have not done in it?" He had provided so much for His people, yet still they turned away.

2. Isaiah 22:12-14—"In that day did the Lord God of hosts call to weeping, and to mourning, and to baldness, and to girding with sackcloth. And, behold, joy and gladness; . . . let us eat and drink; for tomorrow we shall die." God called for weeping—a reflection of His attitude toward Israel's sin—but instead the people had a party.

3. Isaiah 59:12-13—Isaiah said to his people, "Our transgressions are multiplied . . . in transgressing and lying against the Lord, and departing from our God."

D. As Seen in Jeremiah

1. Jeremiah 2:13—God said, "My people have committed two evils: they have forsaken me, the fountain of living waters, and hewed out cisterns, broken cisterns, that can hold no water." Israel had rejected the source of water (God) for broken water pots (idols), which couldn't produce or even contain water.

2. Jeremiah 2:19-20—God declared to Israel, "Thine own wickedness shall correct thee, and thy backslidings shall reprove thee; know, therefore, and see that it is an evil thing and bitter, that thou hast forsaken the Lord, thy God, and that my fear is not in thee, saith the Lord God of hosts. For of old I have broken thy yoke, and burst thy bands; and thou saidst, I will not transgress." God had set them free by leading them out of Egypt. Nevertheless, "Upon every high hill and under every green tree thou wanderest, playing the harlot. Yet I had planted thee a noble vine, wholly a right seed. How, then, art thou turned into the degenerate plant of a strange vine unto me?" (vv. 20-21). God was saying, "What went wrong? How did you become so polluted?"

3. Jeremiah 3:20-22—"Surely, as a wife treacherously departeth from her husband, so have ye dealt treacherously with me, O house of Israel, saith the Lord. A voice was heard upon the high places, weeping, and supplications of the children of Israel; for they have perverted their way, and they have forgotten the Lord, their God. Return, ye backsliding children, and I will heal your backslidings."

4. Jeremiah 15:6—"Thou hast forsaken me, saith the Lord, thou art gone backward; therefore will I stretch out my hand against thee, and destroy thee; I am weary with repenting."

5. Jeremiah 17:13—"O Lord, the hope of Israel, all who forsake thee shall be ashamed, and they who depart from me shall be written in the earth, because they have forsaken the Lord."

The dominant theme in the book of Jeremiah is Israel's defection from God.

Hope for Israel

Though Israel's history is filled with spiritual defections, there is hope for the future. God said to Jeremiah, "They shall be my people, and I will be their God; and I will give them one heart, and one way, that they may fear me forever, for the good of them, and of their children after them; and I will make an everlasting covenant with them, that I will not turn away from doing them good, but I will put my fear in their hearts, that they shall not depart from me" (Jer. 32:38-40). Israel's spiritual defection will end when God's New Covenant with them is fully realized (cf. Jer. 31:27-40).

II. GOD'S SORROW OVER SPIRITUAL DEFECTION

A. Revealed Through Jeremiah

We see God's sorrow through the tears of Jeremiah, who was known as "the weeping prophet."

1. Jeremiah 9:1-2—"Oh, that my head were waters, and mine eyes a fountain of tears, that I might weep day and night for the slain of the daughter of my people! Oh, that I had in the wilderness a lodging place of wayfaring men, that I might leave my people, and go from them!" Jeremiah wanted to go away and be alone to mourn Israel's defection.

2. Jeremiah 14:7-8—"O Lord, though our iniquities testify against us, do it for thy name's sake; for our backslidings are many; we have sinned against thee. . . . Why shouldest thou be like a sojourner in the land, and like a wayfaring man who turneth aside to tarry for a night?" Because Israel was treating God like a stranger, He told Jeremiah, "Thou shalt say this word unto them, Let mine eyes run down with tears night and day, and let them not cease; for the virgin daughter of my people is broken with a great breach, with a very grievous blow" (v. 17).

3. Lamentations 2:11—"Mine eyes do fail with tears, my heart is troubled, my liver is poured upon the earth, for the destruction of the daughter of my people."

Throughout the prophecies of Jeremiah we see the sorrow of God over the defection of His people Israel.

B. Revealed Through Christ

1. He wept over Jerusalem

Luke 19:41 says, "When [Jesus] was come near, he beheld the city, and wept over it." The Greek word translated "wept" doesn't imply merely a gentle tear flowing down the cheek but a great heaving of heart and soul. Then Jesus said to Jerusalem, "If thou hadst known, even thou, at least in this thy day, the things which belong unto thy peace! But now they are hidden from thine eyes. For the days shall come upon thee, that thine enemies shall cast a trench about thee, and compass thee round, and keep thee in on every side, and shall lay thee even with the ground, and thy children within thee; and they shall not leave in thee one stone upon another; because thou knewest not the time of thy visitation" (vv. 42-44).

Although the people in Jerusalem initially received Jesus warmly (Luke 19:37-38; Matt. 21:9-11), He knew they were blind to His purposes and would soon reject Him. His tears show how much God is grieved by those who defect from Him.

The Pain of Defection

Few things sadden me more than remembering people I know who have forsaken God. They claimed to know Christ and love His people but walked away from both. It is most sad when that happens to someone in your own family. I have talked to husbands and wives whose spouses denied their faith and walked out. I have talked to heartbroken parents whose children have turned their backs on Christ. Anyone in ministry has had to deal with similar situations.

2. He was forsaken by His followers

I believe no other portion of Scripture better reveals Jesus' pain over spiritual defection than John 6. Verse 66 says, "From that time many of his disciples went back, and walked no more with him." They proved to be false disciples when they forsook Christ. "Then said Jesus unto the twelve, Will ye also go away?" (v. 67). He turned to His most intimate followers and asked if they would abandon Him as well. "Then Simon Peter answered him, Lord, to whom shall we go? Thou hast the words of eternal life. And we believe and are sure that thou art that Christ, the Son of the living God" (vv. 68-69).

Peter's strong confession must have pleased Jesus, but all twelve were not as committed to Christ as he was. "Jesus answered them, Have not I chosen you twelve, and one of you is a devil? He spoke of Judas Iscariot, the son of Simon; for he it was that should betray him, being one of the twelve" (vv. 70-71). Jesus' own friend would "lift up his heel" against him, as David had prophesied (Ps. 41:9; cf. John 13:18-19). Judas was so trusted by the disciples that he carried the money for the little band of nomads. But he would betray the Lord with a kiss after Jesus called him "friend." I believe the knowledge of Judas's impending defection—though it fit into the sovereign plan of God—was a continual source of anguish for Christ.

Spiritual defection grieves the One who loves us and gave Himself for us. Therefore, we each need to make sure that we are genuine disciples of Christ. May our study affirm our faith and deepen our commitment to obey God's Word.

Focusing on the Facts

1. Define *defection* (see p. 7).
2. How does God feel about those who follow Him for a short time and then forsake Him (see pp. 7-8)?
3. What is David implying in Psalm 18:21 (see pp. 8-9)?

4. God is a _____ who feels the pain of desertion (see p. 9).
5. What did God call for as a reflection of His attitude toward Israel's sin (see p. 9)?
6. What is the dominant theme in the book of Jeremiah (see pp. 10-11)?
7. Whose sadness does Jeremiah's weeping represent (see p. 11)?
8. Why did Jesus weep over Jerusalem (see p. 12)?
9. What do many of Jesus' disciples do in John 6:66? What does that tell us about them (see p. 13)?
10. What was probably a continual source of anguish to Jesus (see p. 13)?

Pondering the Principles

1. Jesus said, "If ye continue in my word, then are ye my disciples indeed" (John 8:31). He identified those who left Him as false disciples who were never truly saved. Consider some other passages that teach perseverance as a proof of true faith: Hebrews 3:14 says, "We are made partakers of Christ, if we hold the beginning of our confidence steadfast unto the end." First John 2:19 says, "They went out from us, but they were not of us; for if they had been of us, they would no doubt have continued with us; but they went out, that they might be made manifest that they were not all of us." And 2 Timothy 2:12 says, "If we deny Him, He also will deny us."

2. In the next two chapters we will study John 6 to see what characterizes those who follow Christ for a time and then leave Him. But before we do, write down some motives and attitudes you think a superficial disciple would have. Why would someone who is not regenerate be attracted to Christianity? Also, write down some reasons you think such a person would turn away from Christ. Finally, describe a true believer. What motives and attitudes would characterize him or her?

2

Marks of a Spiritual Defector—Part 1

Outline

Lesson
 I. He Is Attracted by the Crowd (vv. 1-2)
 II. He Is Fascinated by the Supernatural (vv. 2-13)
   A. Why Jesus Performed Miracles
     1. To test His disciples
     2. To build His disciples' faith
   B. Why the Crowd Followed Christ
 III. He Is Preoccupied with Earthly Things (vv. 14-15)
 IV. He Has No Desire to Worship Christ (vv. 16-21)
 V. He Seeks Personal Prosperity (vv. 22-27)
 VI. He Makes Demands on God (vv. 28-34)
   A. The Demand for Power
   B. The Demand for Proof
   C. The Demand for Provision
 VII. He Doesn't Seek a Personal Relationship with Christ
   (vv. 35-40)

Conclusion

Lesson

Spiritual defection is a recurring theme in Scripture. John 6 helps to explain why many people follow the Lord for a short time and then forsake Him. Verse 66 says, "From that time many of [Jesus'] disciples went back, and walked no more with him." Why did that happen? The preceding verses in this great chapter tell us, revealing some characteristics of those who left Christ.

15

I. HE IS ATTRACTED BY THE CROWD (vv. 1-2)

John 6 begins, "After these things Jesus went over the Sea of Galilee, which is the Sea of Tiberias. And a great multitude followed him." In that huge crowd, the defectors were indistinguishable from the real disciples. "After these things" refers to events of Christ's Galilean ministry omitted by John but recorded in Matthew 4-5, Mark 1-7, and Luke 4-9. During that time, Jesus had taught, healed, cast out demons, and raised the dead—He was the event of a lifetime.

Jesus' popularity attracted many shallow followers who eventually defected. I fear that a similar danger exists in our country today, where Christianity has attained a certain degree of popularity. Professing Christ requires little sacrifice here; we certainly don't have to die for our faith, as some Christians in other countries do. In fact, being identified with Jesus and claiming to be born again may be "in" at times. That kind of environment attracts the spiritual defector. He'll be where the numbers are.

II. HE IS FASCINATED BY THE SUPERNATURAL (vv. 2-13)

Verse 2 says, "A great multitude followed him, because they saw his miracles which he did on those who were diseased."

A. Why Jesus Performed Miracles

1. To test His disciples

After a quiet moment with His disciples (vv. 3-5), Jesus was approached by a massive crowd. Matthew 14:14 tells us He "was moved with compassion toward them, and he healed their sick." That went on all day, and at mealtime the disciples told Christ to send the multitude away so that the people could buy their dinner before it got too late (v. 15).

But Jesus said to Philip, "Where shall we buy bread, that these may eat? And this he said to test him; for he himself knew what he would do" (John 6:5-6). Jesus was testing Philip's faith. He wanted to see if Philip believed He had the power to supply dinner for everyone. Unfortunately, Philip failed the test. He said to

Christ, "Two hundred denarii's worth of bread is not sufficient for them, that every one of them may take a little" (v. 7). Philip was saying they didn't have enough money to feed the people. He didn't even consider that Christ might have something supernatural in mind, even though he had seen all the miracles the Lord had done in Galilee.

Philip wasn't alone in failing the test. Andrew did, too. Verses 8-9 say, "One of his disciples, Andrew, Simon Peter's brother, saith unto him, There is a lad here, who hath five barley loaves and two small fishes; but what are they among so many?" Andrew was the typical pragmatist: he examined the resources and decided there weren't enough.

2. To build His disciples' faith

Jesus then proceeded to bolster Philip and Andrew's weak faith through an incredible miracle. The primary purpose of Jesus' miracles was to build the faith of those who already believed, rather than convince those who didn't. He said, "Make the men sit down. . . . So the men sat down, in number about five thousand" (v. 10). We can assume that five thousand men had five thousand women with them, and perhaps as many as fifteen or twenty thousand children. It was a large crowd! "Jesus took the loaves; and when he had given thanks, he distributed to the disciples, and the disciples to them that were sitting down; and likewise of the fishes as much as they would" (v. 11).

That is a low-key presentation of a monumental miracle. A skeptic might say that everyone took very small bites, but I doubt that. The only way Jesus could have fed all those people was by miraculously creating the food. He showed the disciples He could make much out of little, despite their lack of faith. Aren't you glad His gifts are dispensed according to the riches of His grace (Eph. 1:7), not the poverty of our faith?

Verses 12-13 say, "When they were filled, he said unto his disciples, Gather up the fragments that remain, that nothing be lost. Therefore, they gathered them together, and filled twelve baskets with the fragments of the five barley loaves which remained." Jesus created more than was necessary to feed the people. The Greek word translated "basket" is *kophinos*, from which we get the word *coffin*. The baskets the disciples used to collect the remnants were probably quite large.

B. Why the Crowd Followed Christ

Miracles like that, although intended primarily as faith-builders for the disciples, were the main attraction for the spiritual defectors. Much of the crowd followed Jesus "because they saw his miracles" (v. 2). They could see in His supernatural power the answer to all their problems.

1. Matthew 4:24-25—"His fame went throughout all Syria; and they brought unto him all sick people that were taken with diverse diseases and torments, and those who were possessed with demons, and those who were epileptics, and those who had the palsy; and he healed them. And there followed him great multitudes of people." Jesus' healing ministry attracted many thrill-seekers who wanted to see miracles.

2. Matthew 12:15—"Great multitudes followed him, and he healed them all." That kind of supernatural activity will draw a crowd anywhere.

Many who followed Christ during His ministry were fascinated with the supernatural and preoccupied with how it could be used for their benefit. Today many people are attracted to Christianity because they want miraculous healing, deliverance, and provision. Beware of those seeking signs and wonders (cf. Matt. 16:4); they are likely to defect.

III. HE IS PREOCCUPIED WITH EARTHLY THINGS (vv. 14-15)

Verse 14 says, "Then those men, when they had seen the miracle that Jesus did, said, This is of a truth that prophet that should come into the world." By calling Him "that prophet," the men were affirming that Jesus was the promised Messiah (cf. Deut. 18:15; Acts 3:22-23). Verse 15 says that Jesus "perceived that they would come and take him by force, to make him a king." Rather than bowing before Him in worship and adoration, the people wanted to force Him to become king. Why? Because they wanted Jesus to overthrow the Romans. He then could provide free food for everyone in Israel. *This is it*, they thought. *No more toiling under the hot sun, plowing the field, crushing the grapes, grinding the grain into flour, or slaughtering the animals. We can just sit in the shade and wait for Him to create the next meal!*

Their plans to "take him by force" exemplify a lack of respect for Christ that is prevalent in the church today. Some think Jesus will meet any demand they make of Him. If they want a new house or car, they "name it and claim it." Instead of worshiping Christ, they use Him to get what they want. But He has no time for that kind of carnal enthusiasm: verse 15 says He withdrew from those people. The shallow follower has no sense of the spiritual or the eternal. He lives for today and defects when Christ does not fulfill all his earthly desires.

IV. HE HAS NO DESIRE TO WORSHIP CHRIST (vv. 16-21)

Matthew 14:22 tells us that before Jesus went away to be alone, He commanded the disciples to get into a boat and sail to the other side of the sea. John 6:16-18 says, "When evening was now come, his disciples went down unto the sea, and entered into a boat, and went over the sea toward Capernaum. And it was now dark, and Jesus was not come to them. And the sea arose, by reason of a great wind that blew." With the strong blasts of wind coming from the deep ravines at its northern end, the Sea of Galilee is noted for its sudden and violent storms. One such storm stranded the disciples in the middle of the sea nearly all night. Verse 19 says they only rowed about three or four miles. According to Matthew 14:25, they rowed until the fourth watch of the night, which was between 3:00 and 6:00 A.M. They must have been terrified after rowing all night and getting nowhere.

Then the disciples saw "Jesus walking on the sea, and drawing near unto the boat; and they were afraid. But he saith unto them, It is I; be not afraid" (John 6:19-20). Matthew 14:28-33 describes Peter's near-fatal attempt to walk to Jesus on the water and tells us that the storm ceased when the two entered

19

the boat. "Then they that were in the boat came and worshiped him, saying, Of a truth, thou art the Son of God" (v. 33). John 6:21 says, "They willingly received him into the boat; and immediately the boat was at the land to which they went."

Compare their response with that of the multitude; the crowds never fell down in adoration before Christ or offered Him praise. They didn't come to give but to take. The spiritual defector isn't interested in the reverent worship the disciples offered Christ.

V. HE SEEKS PERSONAL PROSPERITY (vv. 22-27)

"The day following, when the people who stood on the other side of the sea saw that there was no other boat there, except that one into which his disciples were entered, and that Jesus went not with his disciples into the boat, but that his disciples were gone away alone . . . they also took boats and came to Capernaum, seeking for Jesus" (vv. 22-24) A flotilla of ships landed in Capernaum searching for Christ. Dinner had been so good that now the people wanted breakfast!

Food was especially important to those people because their lives centered on agriculture. The free food Jesus could provide was a ticket to instant retirement. Verse 25 says, "When they had found him on the other side of the sea, they said unto him, Rabbi, when camest thou here?" The people had burned off all the calories from the night before by rowing across the sea, so they wanted breakfast. I believe the tone of their question to Jesus was critical, as if to say, "What are you doing over here when you knew we were over there? How dare you!"

Jesus replied, "Verily, verily, I say to you, Ye seek me, not because ye saw the miracles, but because ye did eat of the loaves, and were filled. Labor not for the food which perisheth" (vv. 26-27). The Greek word translated "filled" (*chortazō*) speaks of being gorged or foddered up like an animal. They had eaten to their hearts' content and now wanted more. Those people would have been great candidates for the "prosperity gospel." They were spiritual defectors who had come to Christ for selfish reasons.

VI. HE MAKES DEMANDS ON GOD (vv. 28-34)

In verse 27 Jesus calls the people to salvation, saying, "Labor . . . for that food which endureth unto everlasting life, which the Son of man shall give unto you; for him hath God the Father sealed." However, the multitude was still preoccupied with breakfast. They ignored His challenge to seek what was eternally significant and instead met Him with demands.

A. The Demand for Power

The crowd said to Jesus, "What shall we do, that we might work the works of God?" (v. 28). I believe they wanted the supernatural power Jesus had. They were saying, "We don't want to follow you around all the time to get food. Just tell us how to make it." They were like Simon the sorcerer, who tried to buy the Holy Spirit's power from the apostles (Acts 8:18-19).

B. The Demand for Proof

Jesus answered them by saying, "This is the work of God, that ye believe on him whom he hath sent" (v. 29). But the people responded, "What sign showest thou, then, that we may see, and believe thee? What dost thou work?" (v. 30). They were still pushing for breakfast, saying, "Do a miracle. Prove that we should believe in you." But they didn't need more proof. They had already seen Jesus raise the dead, heal the sick, cast out demons, and feed thousands. They didn't want to believe—they wanted more food. So they demanded that He prove himself by performing another miracle.

Thrill-seekers can never get enough signs, wonders, and miracles—they always want more. Today the promise of more and greater miracles sustains many shallow disciples for a time. But when they realize that what are advertised as miracles really aren't, they defect.

C. The Demand for Provision

In verse 31 we see the crowd still trying to goad Jesus into creating more food: "Our fathers did eat manna in the desert; as it is written, He gave them bread from heaven to eat." Moses had given manna to millions of people every day for years, they thought, so if Jesus was the Messiah He should at least do as much as Moses. The self-seeking crowd wanted no less than a perpetual food supply. Jesus said to them, "Verily, verily, I say unto you, Moses gave you not that bread from heaven; but my Father giveth you the true bread from heaven. For the bread of God is he who cometh down from heaven, and giveth life unto the world" (vv. 32-33). Manna was physical bread that couldn't prevent death, but the true Bread is spiritual and gives eternal life.

Jesus' profound words were lost on the crowd, however. "Then said they unto him, Lord, evermore give us this bread" (v. 34). They were demanding food that would permanently satisfy their physical hunger, not realizing that He was offering Himself to meet their spiritual needs.

VII. HE DOESN'T SEEK A PERSONAL RELATIONSHIP WITH CHRIST (vv. 35-40)

In verses 35-36 Jesus says, "I am the bread of life; he that cometh to me shall never hunger, and he that believeth on me shall never thirst. But I said unto you that ye also have seen me, and believe not." Jesus Christ Himself is the bread of life. The true disciple seeks to know Him, but the defector seeks only what He can give.

Jesus' Refuge in God's Sovereignty

The crowd's preoccupation with physical things and disinterest in spiritual things must have saddened Christ tremendously. But in verses 37-39 He derives comfort from God's sovereignty, declaring, "All that the Father giveth me shall come to me; and him that cometh to me I will in no wise cast out. For I came down from heaven, not to do mine own will but the will of him that sent me. And this is the Father's will who hath sent me, that of all that he hath given me I should lose nothing, but should raise it up again at the last day." Jesus found comfort in knowing that their unbelief could not thwart the eternal plan of God. Any servant of God can find comfort in that fact as well. When our hearts ache because people reject Christ, we can be encouraged by the promise that all the Father gives will come to Christ.

Jesus said, "This is the will of him that sent me, that everyone who seeth the Son, and believeth on him, may have everlasting life; and I will raise him up at the last day" (v. 40). The use of the word *everyone* shows that the truth of God's sovereign election does not preclude a wide invitation to salvation. Even though only those whom the Father draws will accept it (v. 44), we're to extend the invitation to all. And Christ promised that no one who comes to Him will be turned away (v. 37).

Jesus was speaking of a personal relationship when He said, "Come to me." All true disciples pursue that relationship. They seek the Savior, not just what He can give to them. Defectors, however, have no desire for a relationship.

Conclusion

Those who turn their backs on Christ and walk away from Him (John 6:66) are often drawn by the crowd, fascinated with the supernatural, and preoccupied with earthly things. They have no desire for worship, seek personal prosperity, make demands on God, and do not hunger for a personal relationship with Christ. All who follow Christ should examine their motives for doing so. Only a genuine relationship with Him can prevent spiritual defection.

Focusing on the Facts

1. Why was Jesus so popular during His ministry in Galilee (see p. 16)?
2. Why did the multitude follow Christ (John 6:2; see p. 16)?
3. Why did Jesus ask Philip where to buy bread (John 6:5-6; see p. 16)?
4. What was the primary purpose of Jesus' miracles (see p. 17)?
5. About how many people might Jesus have fed (see p. 17)?
6. When the people called Jesus "that prophet" (John 6:14), what were they saying about Him (see p. 18)?
7. Why did the people want to make Jesus a king (see p. 19)?
8. What did the disciples do when Jesus entered the boat after walking on the water (Matt. 14:33; see p. 20)?

9. Why was food especially important to the people living in Christ's day (see p. 20)?
10. What three demands did the people make upon Christ (John 6:28-34; see p. 21)?
11. What doctrine of God did Christ find comfort in? Why (John 6:37-40; see p. 22)?
12. What was Jesus speaking of when He said, "Come to me" (John 6:37; see p. 23)?

Pondering the Principles

1. Consider how the marks of a spiritual defector might apply to the church today. Write down some thoughts in response to the following questions: Is it possible for unsaved people to be lost in the crowd at many churches? What kinds of miraculous activity do some Christians claim to be experiencing today, and how might that attract unbelievers to the church? What earthly things offered by the church might attract them? Is it possible to attend church without worshiping God? How could being involved in a church help someone gain personal prosperity? What are some demands church people make on God? And, is it possible to be active in a church without knowing Christ personally?

2. Although Jesus found comfort in God's sovereignty, many Christians avoid that doctrine. They fear that believing in election will remove any incentive for evangelism or other ministry. J. I. Packer corrects that misconception in his helpful book *Evangelism and the Sovereignty of God* (Downers Grove: InterVarsity, 1961): "Far from making evangelism pointless, the sovereignty of God in grace is the one thing that prevents evangelism from being pointless. For it creates the possibility—indeed, the certainty—that evangelism will be fruitful. Apart from it, there is not even a possibility of evangelism being fruitful . . . because of the spiritual inability of man in sin. . . . [We] have every reason to be bold, and free, and natural, and hopeful of success. For God can give His truth an effectiveness that you and I cannot give it. God can make His truth triumphant to the conversion of the most seemingly hardened unbeliever. You and I will never write off anyone as hopeless and beyond the reach of God if we believe in the sovereignty of His grace" (pp. 106, 118-19).

3
Marks of a Spiritual Defector—Part 2

Outline

Review
I. He Is Attracted by the Crowd (vv. 1-2)
II. He Is Fascinated by the Supernatural (vv. 2-13)
III. He Is Preoccupied with Earthly Things (vv. 14-15)
IV. He Has No Desire to Worship Christ (vv. 16-21)
V. He Seeks Personal Prosperity (vv. 22-27)
VI. He Makes Demands on God (vv. 28-34)
VII. He Doesn't Seek a Personal Relationship with Christ (vv. 35-40)

Lesson
VIII. He Speaks Privately Against the Truth (vv. 41-44)
IX. He Has No Hunger for Divine Truth (vv. 45-50)
X. He Has No Hunger for True Salvation (vv. 51-59)
   A. True Salvation Involves Appropriating Christ
   B. True Salvation Involves Becoming One with Christ

Conclusion
A. The Response of the False Disciples
   1. They were offended by Jesus' teaching
   2. They stopped following Him
B. The Response of the True Disciples

Review

I. HE IS ATTRACTED BY THE CROWD (vv. 1-2; see p. 16)

II. HE IS FASCINATED BY THE SUPERNATURAL (vv. 2-13; see pp. 16-18)

III. HE IS PREOCCUPIED WITH EARTHLY THINGS (vv. 14-15; see pp. 18-19)

IV. HE HAS NO DESIRE TO WORSHIP CHRIST (vv. 16-21; see pp. 19-20)

V. HE SEEKS PERSONAL PROSPERITY (vv. 22-27; see p. 20)

VI. HE MAKES DEMANDS ON GOD (vv. 28-34; see pp. 21-22)

VII. HE DOESN'T SEEK A PERSONAL RELATIONSHIP WITH CHRIST (vv. 35-40; see pp. 22-23)

Lesson

VIII. HE SPEAKS PRIVATELY AGAINST THE TRUTH (vv. 41-44)

Those who come to Christ seeking personal gain appear to love the church when they are in it but tend to criticize and mock it when outside. John 6:41-42 says, "The Jews then murmured at him, because he said, I am the bread that came down from heaven. And they said, Is not this Jesus, the son of Joseph, whose father and mother we know? How is it, then, that he saith, I came down from heaven?" They mocked Jesus privately, thinking He couldn't hear. But He rebuked them, saying, "Murmur not among yourselves" (v. 43). Then He repeated His emphasis on God's sovereignty (v. 39), saying, "No man can come to me, except the Father, who hath sent me, draw him; and I will raise him up at the last day" (v. 44).

IX. HE HAS NO HUNGER FOR DIVINE TRUTH (vv. 45-50)

In verse 45 Jesus quotes Isaiah 54:13: "It is written in the prophets, And they shall all be taught of God. Every man, therefore, that hath heard, and hath learned of the Father, cometh unto me." All who come to Christ have been taught by God, which is synonymous with being drawn by the Father (v. 44). God's sovereign calling is always connected with understanding His truth. True disciples come to Christ to learn, but the spiritual defector desires only personal prosperity and self-aggrandizement.

In verse 46 Jesus says, "Not that any man hath seen the Father, except he who is of God; he hath seen the Father." Because Jesus had just mentioned their being taught by the Father (v. 45), He didn't want them to think anyone could actually see the living God in this life. He went on to say, "He that believeth on me hath everlasting life. I am that bread of life. Your fathers did eat manna in the wilderness, and are dead. This is the bread that cometh down from heaven, that a man may eat of it, and not die" (vv. 47-50). Christ repeatedly offered Himself to the multitude, but they weren't interested. They had no desire to understand divine reality.

X. HE HAS NO HUNGER FOR TRUE SALVATION (vv. 51-59)

A. True Salvation Involves Appropriating Christ

In verse 51 Jesus says, "I am the living bread that came down from heaven; if any man eat of this bread, he shall live forever; and the bread that I will give is my flesh, which I will give for the life of the world." He was saying you can have eternal life by receiving Him into your life personally. Jesus likened that appropriation to eating bread. You can sniff bread, admire it, analyze it, philosophize about it, and even eulogize it; but you won't derive any benefit from it until you eat it. Likewise, you won't receive any eternal benefit from Christ until you take Him into your life.

Verse 52 says, "The Jews, therefore, strove among themselves, saying, How can this man give us his flesh to eat?" They mocked what Jesus said, showing their abysmal ignorance. "Is He teaching cannibalism?" they asked. They couldn't understand His simple metaphor. He obviously wasn't talking about His literal flesh because He had just said He would give His flesh for the life of the world (v. 51). Did they think He was silly enough to imply that He had enough flesh to feed the whole world?

Christ was talking about a spiritual reception, or appropriation, of all that He is, saying, "He who eateth my flesh, and drinketh my blood, hath eternal life; and I will raise him up at the last day. For my flesh is food indeed, and my blood is drink indeed" (vv. 54-55). He may have been referring to His incarnation when He said, "My flesh" and to His death on the cross when He said, "My blood." Those who embrace His person and His work will be raised from the dead as He was raised.

B. True Salvation Involves Becoming One with Christ

In verse 56 Jesus says, "He that eateth my flesh, and drinketh my blood, dwelleth in me, and I in him." When we believe in Christ, we become one with Him. We also receive His divine life: "As the living Father hath sent me, and I live by the Father, so he that eateth me, even he shall live by me" (v. 57). Paul echoed that same thought: "I am crucified with Christ: nevertheless I live; yet not I, but Christ liveth in me; and the life which I now live in the flesh I live by the faith of the Son of God, who loved me and gave himself for me" (Gal. 2:20). And the life we receive from Christ is eternal, for Jesus said, "Not as your fathers did eat manna, and are dead; he that eateth of this bread shall live forever" (John 6:58).

Salvation is a relationship that true disciples long for but false disciples ignore.

Comparing Salvation to Eating

1. Both are necessary

To derive any nutritional benefit from bread, we must eat it. We can look at it, squeeze it, and taste it—but it will do nothing for us until we eat it. The same is true of Christ. We can admire

Him from a distance, talk about Him, and say we believe in Him—but only when we receive Him into our own lives as Lord and Savior will we have eternal life.

2. Both are responses to a felt need

It's wonderful to eat when you're hungry, but it's repulsive to eat when you're not. The person with no appetite for things divine is stuffed with the food that perishes (John 6:27), so the thought of the true Bread is nauseating to him. His sin leaves no room for Christ. It's not until a person is broken regarding his sin, awakened to his lost condition, and aware of the deep void in his soul that he will eagerly eat the true Bread.

3. Both require personal involvement

No one can eat for you—it's something you must do for yourself. I sometimes get so busy I wish I could have someone else do my eating so that I wouldn't have to take the time. But that doesn't work. Likewise, each of us must personally appropriate Christ to be saved.

Christ chose a marvelously rich analogy when He said we must eat His flesh and drink His blood to be saved.

Conclusion

A. The Response of the False Disciples

1. They were offended by Jesus' teaching

"Many, therefore, of his disciples, when they had heard this, said, This is an hard saying. Who can hear it?" (v. 60). Many of Jesus' followers, who were not necessarily true believers, found His teaching offensive. Why? Partly because of His metaphoric language but also because of His narrowness: He had been saying that He alone was the source of spiritual life. "When Jesus knew in himself that his disciples murmured at it, he said unto them, Doth this offend you? What if ye shall see the Son of man ascend up where he was before?" (vv. 61-62).

2. They stopped following Him

> Jesus said, "It is the spirit that giveth life; the flesh profiteth nothing. The words that I speak unto you, they are spirit, and they are life. But there are some of you that believe not. For Jesus knew from the beginning who they were that believed not, and who should betray him" (vv. 63-64). Jesus was omniscient. He knew who the defectors in the crowd were. How deeply that knowledge must have hurt His perfect soul! So He leaned on God's sovereignty again, saying, "Therefore said I unto you that no man can come unto me, except it were given unto him of my Father" (v. 65; cf. v. 44).

> Verse 66 says, "From that time many of his disciples went back, and walked no more with him." I believe Jesus' heart was broken over the defection of those fickle disciples. Though He trusted in God's sovereignty, He felt great pain over their unbelief.

B. The Response of the True Disciples

> "Then said Jesus unto the twelve, Will ye also go away?" (v. 67). The pathos in that verse is especially clear in the Greek text. Jesus was saying, "You won't also go away, will you?" Peter responded on behalf of all the genuine disciples still remaining: "Lord, to whom shall we go? Thou hast the words of eternal life. And we believe and are sure that thou art that Christ, the Son of the living God" (vv. 68-69). They knew the Lord's words were spiritual, and they followed Him because they were concerned with heavenly things. What a difference from the rest of the crowd! By the grace of God, the real disciples sought to worship Christ and have a personal relationship with Him.

However, not even all of the twelve were genuine disciples. Verses 70-71 say, "Jesus answered them, Have not I chosen you twelve, and one of you is a devil? He spoke of Judas Iscariot, the son of Simon; for he it was that should betray him, being one of the twelve." Whereas some false disciples defect early, others, like Judas, remain around Christ for quite some time. Unfortunately, Judas was not the only one who was close to Christ and then turned against Him. Many throughout history have joined him in betraying the Son of God. And every defection grieves His heart.

Focusing on the Facts

1. What three marks of a spiritual defector do we see in John 6:41-59 (see pp. 26-28)?
2. How did Jesus describe God's sovereign call (John 6:39, 44; see pp. 26-27)?
3. What did Jesus mean when He said, "If any man eat of this bread, he shall live forever" (John 6:51; see p. 27)?
4. Salvation is a _____ that true disciples long for (see p. 28).
5. Why do some people have no hunger for spiritual truth (see p. 29)?
6. Why did many of Jesus' followers find His teaching offensive (see p. 29)?
7. What did the real disciples seek in following Christ (see p. 30)?

Pondering the Principles

1. We noted that Jesus used eating as an analogy for salvation. Consider how that truth might apply to a philosophy of evangelism. What are some ways to identify people who are spiritually hungry? Where are some places you might go to find them? And how do you think they could be attracted to your church, your home, or some other place where they could be given answers?

2. Look back over the last two chapters and examine yourself in light of what you've learned. Are any of the marks of a spiritual defector true of you? Are you, for instance, attracted to a crowd, or would you gladly serve in a church of twenty people if God called you? Do you expend more effort in earthly pursuits or in furthering God's kingdom? Remember, Christ taught that many who call Him Lord and are busy in His service will be excluded from heaven because they do not truly know Him (Matt. 7:21-23). An examination of your motives will reveal if you are a true disciple of Christ.

4
The Danger of Defection

Outline

Introduction
A. The Old Testament Passages
   1. God's judgment on cities
   2. God's judgment on individuals
B. The New Testament Parallel

Lesson
I. Two Responses to the Gospel
  A. Receiving Christ
    1. The invitation to receive Christ
    2. The characteristics of true conversion
      a) A sincere heart
      b) A confident faith
      c) A cleansed conscience
      d) A washed body
      e) Perseverance
      f) A love of the fellowship
  B. Rejecting Christ
    1. The reasons people defect
      a) Persecution
      b) False teaching
      c) Temptation
      d) Worldliness
      e) Neglect
      f) A hardened heart
    2. The unbroken pattern of sin
II. Two Results of Defection
  A. There Is No Other Sacrifice for Sins
  B. There Is Certain and Severe Judgment Awaiting

1. For trampling the Son of God underfoot
2. For regarding the blood of the covenant as unclean
3. For insulting the Spirit of grace

Conclusion

Introduction

One of the responsibilities of a pastor is to warn people, and something we all need to be warned about is the danger of spiritual defection. Some people come close to having their sins forgiven and possessing eternal life but turn and fall away without being truly saved. Their apostasy has serious and eternal consequences.

A. The Old Testament Passages

The book of Deuteronomy makes clear how God feels about spiritual defection.

1. God's judgment on cities

In Deuteronomy 13:12-17 Moses says to Israel, "If you hear in one of your cities, which the Lord your God is giving you to live in, anyone saying that some worthless men have gone out from among you and have seduced the inhabitants of their city, saying, 'Let us go and serve other gods' (whom you have not known), then you shall investigate and search out and inquire thoroughly. And if it is true and the matter established that this abomination has been done among you, you shall surely strike the inhabitants of that city with the edge of the sword, utterly destroying it and all that is in it and its cattle with the edge of the sword. Then you shall gather all its booty into the middle of its open square and burn the city and all its booty with fire as a whole burnt offering to the Lord your God; and it shall be a ruin forever. It shall never be rebuilt. And nothing from that which is put under the ban shall cling to your hand, in order that the Lord may turn from His burning anger and show mercy to you, and have compassion on you and make you increase, just as He has sworn to your fathers, if you will listen to the voice of the Lord your God, keeping all

His commandments which I am commanding you to-day, and doing what is right in the sight of the Lord your God."

The Israelites were told that if someone led one of their cities in worshiping false gods, everyone and everything associated with that city should be completely destroyed. Only then would God's anger be turned away. That's how strongly He feels about spiritual defection.

2. God's judgment on individuals

Deuteronomy 17:2-6 says, "If there is found in your midst, in any of your towns, which the Lord your God is giving you, a man or a woman who does what is evil in the sight of the Lord your God, by transgressing His covenant, and has gone and served other gods and worshiped them, or the sun or the moon or any of the heavenly host, which I have not commanded, and if it is told you and you have heard of it, then you shall inquire thoroughly. And behold, if it is true and the thing certain that this detestable thing has been done in Israel, then you shall bring out that man or that woman who has done this evil deed, to your gates, that is, the man or the women, and you shall stone them to death. On the evidence of two witnesses or three witnesses, he who is to die shall be put to death."

If a city turned from what it knew to be true, it was to be burned and all its people slaughtered. If an individual defected, he was to be stoned to death. God wants people to understand how serious it is to know the truth and depart from it.

B. The New Testament Parallel

Hebrews 10 is the New Testament parallel to the passages in Deuteronomy. Verses 28-29 say, "Anyone who has set aside the Law of Moses dies without mercy on the testimony of two or three witnesses. How much severer punishment do you think he will deserve who has trampled under foot the Son of God, and has regarded as unclean the blood of the covenant by which he was sanctified, and has insulted the Spirit of grace?" Those who reject the Son of God are in even worse danger than those who defected during Moses' time.

Lesson

I. TWO RESPONSES TO THE GOSPEL

Those who have heard and understood the gospel can either believe or reject it. God promises eternal heaven to those who believe in His Son, and eternal hell to those who reject Him. In Hebrews 10 the writer has clearly been discussing the gospel. Verse 10 says, "We have been sanctified through the offering of the body of Jesus Christ once for all." Verse 12 says that Christ "offered one sacrifice for sins for all time." And verse 14 says that "by one offering He has perfected for all time those who are sanctified." Those verses focus on the saving work of Christ on the cross, which is the essence of the gospel.

The readers of this epistle fell into two categories: those who believed to salvation and those who rejected to damnation. In both cases they knew and understood the gospel. Those who rejected it had trampled the Son of God underfoot and regarded the blood of the covenant as unclean; they had also insulted the Holy Spirit because they understood who the Son was, knew what He had done on the cross, and had seen the Spirit working in their midst. People who know the gospel and reject Christ have a much more severe punishment reserved for them than those under the Old Covenant. Thus, knowing the gospel brings about either the greatest blessing or the most severe curse.

A. Receiving Christ

1. The invitation to receive Christ

Verses 19-22 say, "Since therefore, brethren, we have confidence to enter the holy place by the blood of Jesus, by a new and living way which He inaugurated for us through the veil, that is, His flesh, and since we have a great priest over the house of God, let us draw near." "Draw near" is an invitation to salvation. It is the main verb and primary thrust of the sentence. The idea is repeated in James 4:8, which says, "Draw near to God and He will draw near to you."

Verses 19-21 tell us that our great High Priest has cleared the way into the presence of God through His sacrifice. God is accessible to us because of Christ. Therefore we are to "draw near."

2. The characteristics of true conversion

Verses 22-25 explain what it means to draw near to God: "Let us draw near with a sincere heart in full assurance of faith, having our hearts sprinkled clean from an evil conscience and our bodies washed with pure water. Let us hold fast the confession of our hope without wavering, for He who promised is faithful; and let us consider how to stimulate one another to love and good deeds, not forsaking our own assembling together, as is the habit of some, but encouraging one another; and all the more, as you see the day drawing near."

a) A sincere heart

Drawing near with a sincere heart means coming to God with the right motive, which is a desire to experience the forgiveness of sin. A sincere heart grows out of the soil of repentance and confession. It feels a desperate need for the salvation that only God can provide.

b) A confident faith

True conversion also means having full confidence in the gospel. We must come to God affirming without equivocation that His Word is true. Jeremiah wrote about coming to God with your whole heart (Jer. 3:10; 24:7). It means committing everything to Him because you have a certain desperation about your sin and you fully believe the gospel.

Faith like that is a gift from God, not a human work (Eph. 2:8-9). It is the Holy Spirit who convicts the world of sin (John 16:9) and grants repentance (2 Tim. 2:25).

c) A cleansed conscience

When we draw near to God in genuine repentance and confident faith, He then cleanses our conscience, giving us a new sense of moral responsibility. An unregenerate person has a skewed conscience or a warped sense of moral responsibility. But when he draws near to God, he receives a right set of values.

d) A washed body

"Having . . . our bodies washed with pure water" (v. 22) is a figurative expression alluding to a bride's ceremonial bath prior to her wedding—a symbol of her purity. It means that God not only puts a new sense of moral responsibility within us but also washes us of all the filth we accumulated while we were living by our evil conscience. He removes the stain of our sin.

e) Perseverance

Verse 23 says, "Let us hold fast the confession of our hope without wavering, for He who promised is faithful." True disciples continue in the faith. Jesus said, "If ye continue in my word, then are ye my disciples indeed" (John 8:31, KJV*). We can persevere because our faithful God has promised to keep us.

f) A love of the fellowship

Verses 24-25 say, "Let us consider how to stimulate one another to love and good deeds, not forsaking our own assembling together, as is the habit of some, but encouraging one another; and all the more, as you see the day drawing near." When true conversion occurs, there will be a desire to meet with other believers to build one another up for God's service.

The writer of Hebrews was pleading with those who knew the gospel but had not truly come to Christ. Perhaps you

*King James Version.

have heard and understood the gospel, affirmed that it is true, and even identified with the church; but something holds you back from committing your life to Christ. If so, I say to you what the writer of Hebrews said: Please draw near to God while you still can, because the most severe punishment in hell will be experienced by those who knew the truth and rejected it.

B. Rejecting Christ

In verse 26 we encounter such defectors.

1. The reasons people defect

Before we look at the text, I would like to suggest some things that pull people away or lead them to defect.

a) Persecution

When there is a high price to pay for naming the name of Christ, it is highly probable that some will defect. Jesus said that in the last days "they will deliver you to tribulation, and will kill you, and you will be hated by all nations on account of My name" (Matt. 24:9). That's why "most people's love will grow cold" (v. 12). People will fall away because the cost of following Christ is too high. They will admit the gospel is true but refuse to make the sacrifice required.

b) False teaching

Second Timothy 4:3-4 says that "the time will come when [people] will not endure sound doctrine; but wanting to have their ears tickled, they will accumulate for themselves teachers in accordance to their own desires; and will turn away their ears from the truth, and will turn aside to myths." Many times people affirm the gospel but then are allured by some kind of cult. That's reminiscent of the worthless men in Deuteronomy 13 who say, "Let us go and serve other gods" (v. 13).

c) Temptation

Sometimes love of sin can draw people away before they fully commit themselves to Christ. They may feel a longing for forgiveness and be on the verge of genuine repentance, but then temptation comes and they love their sin too much to continue toward Him. When they begin to understand the light, some decide they love the darkness better (cf. John 3:19).

d) Worldliness

In the parable of the soils, Jesus talked about "the ones who have heard, and as they go on their way they are choked with worries and riches and pleasures of this life, and bring no fruit to maturity" (Luke 8:14). In 2 Timothy 4:10 Paul says, "Demas, having loved this present world, has deserted me."

e) Neglect

Hebrews 2:3 says, "How shall we escape if we neglect so great a salvation?" Some people, though the opportunity for salvation has been presented to them repeatedly, simply neglect it.

f) A hardened heart

Hebrews 3:12-13 says, "Take care, brethren, lest there should be in any one of you an evil, unbelieving heart, in falling away from the living God . . . lest any one of you be hardened." If someone repeatedly sits under the message of the gospel without responding properly, his heart will grow harder and harder.

2. The unbroken pattern of sin

Verse 26 says, "If we go on sinning willfully after receiving the knowledge of the truth . . ." An unregenerate person is characterized by an unbroken pattern of sin. A Christian does sin, but the pattern of his life is righteousness, and his deepest desire is to be free from sin. But unsaved people continually sin, and they do so willingly. Notice also that they have already received the knowledge of truth. They know the gospel of Christ but turn their backs on Him to pursue sin.

How Close Can Defectors Get?

It's alarming to see how close some people can get to true faith and still be false disciples.

1. To the point of being enlightened

   Hebrews 10:32 says, "Remember the former days, when, after being enlightened." The writer didn't say they were converted. He said they were enlightened, which means they understood the gospel.

2. To the point of being persecuted

   The readers of Hebrews had "endured a great conflict of sufferings, partly, by being made a public spectacle through reproaches and tribulations, and partly by becoming sharers with those who were so treated" (vv. 32-33). Apparently, some of the unbelievers were so closely identified with the church that they were persecuted along with the true believers.

3. To the point of participating in ministry

   Verse 34 says, "You showed sympathy to the prisoners." The spiritual defectors did the same compassionate things that true believers did.

Many of the Hebrews came close to true belief, but verse 39 describes them as "those who shrink back to destruction." And they didn't fall away because of weakness or ignorance—they did so willingly, understanding the truth (v. 26).

II. TWO RESULTS OF DEFECTION

The results are frightening for those who outwardly identify with the church without being genuine disciples and then fall away. Verses 26-27 tell us two results of sinning willfully after receiving a knowledge of the truth.

41

A. There Is No Other Sacrifice for Sins

Sacrifices were continually offered in the Old Testament period, but Christ's death ended the need for that practice. His sacrifice was the one offering needed to open the way to God (v. 12), so when someone rejects Him there is no other provision for sin. There is no salvation in any other name (Acts 4:12). That's why Hebrews 6:4-6 says it is impossible to renew to repentance those who know all about Christ and fall away. They have rejected the only sacrifice available to mankind for redemption.

B. There Is Certain and Severe Judgment Awaiting

Spiritual defectors have only "a certain terrifying expectation of judgment, and the fury of a fire which will consume the adversaries" (v. 27). There's no sacrifice for them, but they will receive judgment. And it is reserved for those who looked most like friends but turned out to be enemies. Judas Iscariot is the chief example of that company. Jesus taught that there will be degrees of punishment in hell(cf. Luke 12:47-48). If you have been favored with the knowledge of the gospel and have feigned love for Christ but have turned your back on Him, you have placed on the cheek of Jesus a Judas kiss. You will end in the same place as that betrayer unless you repent.

Second Thessalonians 1:7-8 speaks further of the fire mentioned above: "The Lord Jesus shall be revealed from heaven with His mighty angels in flaming fire, dealing out retribution to whose who do not know God and to those who do not obey the gospel of our Lord Jesus."

Hebrews 10:28-29 says, "Anyone who has set aside the Law of Moses dies without mercy on the testimony of two or three witnesses. How much severer punishment do you think he will deserve who has trampled under foot the Son of God, and has regarded as unclean the blood of the covenant by which he [Christ] was sanctified, and has insulted the Spirit of grace?" God will deal with today's spiritual defector much more strongly than defectors in Old Testament times. Our text gives three reasons for such severe punishment.

1. For trampling the Son of God underfoot

    The phrase "Son of God" describes Christ in His exaltation. He has been given a name above all names so that "every tongue should confess that Jesus Christ is Lord, to the glory of God the Father" (Phil. 2:11). However, those who reject Him are calling the most worthy object worthless. They are like swine trampling pearls (Matt. 7:6). Rejecting Christ is a sin against the Father who sent Him.

2. For regarding the blood of the covenant as unclean

    The perfect, spotless Lamb of God shed His blood as the final offering for sin. Those who defect are regarding that sacrificial death as insignificant and therefore unclean. They despise the Father by trampling His Son and despise the Son by counting His blood as unclean.

3. For insulting the Spirit of grace

    Those who reject the gospel offend the entire Trinity. The Holy Spirit is the One who enables people to understand the gospel. So when someone understands it and rejects it, he or she is insulting the Spirit.

Be assured that God will judge those who trample, ignore, or insult Him, "for we know Him who said, 'Vengeance is Mine, I will repay.' And again, 'The Lord will judge His people.' It is a terrifying thing to fall into the hands of the living God" (Heb. 10:30-31; cf. Deut. 32:35-36). Be warned that if you know the truth and are lured away from it, you are in danger of severe judgment at the hands of the living God. Be willing to pray, as the psalmist did, "Enlighten my eyes, lest I sleep the sleep of death" (Ps. 13:3).

Conclusion

Hebrews 10:19-39 is a serious passage of Scripture. People who know the gospel and have not believed must be warned about the consequences. We who believe must be compelled to faithfulness. If you know the Lord Jesus Christ, thank Him for His grace, and ask Him to show you someone who may be in danger of defecting so that you can help that person. If you don't know Christ or have held back in some way from committing your life to Him, cry out to God right now, saying, "O God, save me. I give my life to You." As 2 Corinthians 6:2 says, "Behold, now is 'the acceptable time,' behold, now is 'the day of salvation'" (cf. Isa. 49:8). Come to Christ with a sincere heart and confident faith, asking the Spirit of God to work in your life.

Focusing on the Facts

1. What did God tell the Israelites to do to a city that defected spiritually (Deut. 13:12-17)? To a defecting individual (Deut. 17:2-6; see pp. 34-35)?
2. What is the New Testament parallel to the passages in Deuteronomy on defection (see p. 35)?
3. What are the two possible responses to the gospel (see p. 36)?
4. What does "draw near" in Hebrews 10:22 mean (see p. 36)?
5. List some characteristics of true conversion (Heb. 10:22-25; see pp. 37-38).
6. List some reasons people might fail to believe in Christ after understanding the gospel (see pp. 39-40).
7. Unsaved people _____ sin, and they do so _____ (see pp. 40-41).
8. Name some things that might make defectors look like true believers (Heb. 10:32-34; see p. 41).
9. What are two results of spiritual defection (Heb. 10:26-27; p. 42)?
10. Name a passage in which Jesus taught degrees of punishment (see p. 42).
11. Who will receive the retribution of fire when Christ comes with His angels (2 Thess. 1:7-8; see p. 42)?
12. Those who reject the gospel offend the entire _____ (see p. 43).
13. We who believe must be compelled to _____ by Hebrews 10:19-39 (see p. 43).

Pondering the Principles

1. Since perseverance is proof of true faith (see p. 38), is it possible to know we are saved? Yes, we can have assurance by trusting in God's promise to sovereignly preserve us. As we exercised faith in God's saving work when we first came to Christ, we now exercise faith in His preserving work. Paul wrote to the Philippians, "I am confident of this very thing, that He who began a good work in you will perfect it until the day of Christ Jesus" (Phil. 1:6). Jude wrote that God "is able to keep you from stumbling, and to make you stand in the presence of His glory blameless with great joy" (v. 24). So if you have made the proper commitment to Christ, you can be assured that the Holy Spirit will enable you to persevere. Thus you can say with Paul, "I know whom I have believed and I am convinced that He is able to guard what I have entrusted to Him until that day" (2 Tim. 1:12).

2. Examine yourself according to the characteristics of true conversion listed in Hebrews 10:22-25 (see pp. 37-38). Have you come to God with a sincere heart, or with motives other than a longing for forgiveness and fellowship with Him? Have you come with confident faith in the gospel, or are there things you find hard to believe? Has your conscience been cleansed by God, or do you sin without remorse? Are you persevering in the faith, or did you make a shallow commitment to Christ that faded away with time? And do you love the fellowship of Christian people, or would you rather be with unbelievers? If those questions leave you with doubts about your relationship to God, repent and draw near to Him immediately in light of the punishment reserved for those who know the truth but neglect it (cf. Heb. 3:12).

Scripture Index

Topical Index

"Prosperity Gospel." *See* Materialism

Salvation
  assurance of. *See* Assurance of salvation
  characteristics of true, 37-39, 45
  compared to eating. *See* Eating

hunger for. *See* Hunger, spiritual
Sovereignty of God, the
  evangelism and, 24
  refuge of, 22-23, 26-27
Supernatural, fascination with the, 16-18

Worship, not desiring to, 19-20